The Gaining Knowledge from What Happens Next Workbook

Learning Points by Max Lucado's Book

Kaca kore

Disclaimer:

This workbook is an independent publication created to enhance the understanding and application of concepts discussed in *What Happens Next: A Traveler's Guide Through the End of This Age* by Max Lucado. It is not a substitute for the original book, and its contents are intended for educational purposes only. The exercises, summaries, and reflections provided here are designed to facilitate personal reflection and learning. Readers are encouraged to refer to the original book for a complete understanding of the author's perspectives. This workbook does not provide theological, legal, or professional advice. For specific concerns, readers should consult with qualified professionals.

Table of content

Chapter 1: Understanding God's Eternal Plan: The Foundations of Faith

Summary and Key Takeaways

Understanding God's eternal plan is the cornerstone of Christian faith. This chapter explores the fundamental beliefs that underpin our understanding of God's purpose for humanity and the world. At the heart of this plan is the belief that God created humanity to live in relationship with Him, and that this relationship is ultimately fulfilled through Jesus Christ.

God's eternal plan is not a mystery but has been revealed through the Bible. From Genesis to Revelation, the Bible outlines God's purpose: to create a people who would know Him, love Him, and serve Him forever. This plan includes the creation, the fall of humanity, the promise of redemption through Christ, and the ultimate restoration of all things.

One key takeaway from this chapter is the understanding that God's plan is sovereign and unchangeable. Despite the chaos and uncertainty in the world, God's purposes will prevail. This offers believers a sense of security and hope, knowing that God is in control and that His plan is for the ultimate good of those who love Him.

Another takeaway is the recognition of humanity's role in God's plan. We are not passive observers but active participants in His divine purposes. Through faith in Christ, believers are called to live out their faith, share the gospel, and participate in the advancement of God's kingdom on earth.

Real-Life Case Studies

To understand how God's eternal plan unfolds in real life, we can look at the stories of key biblical figures and how their lives reflected God's purposes. For example, the life of Abraham demonstrates how God calls individuals into a covenant relationship and uses them to fulfill His purposes. Abraham was called to leave his homeland and follow God, trusting in His promises. Despite challenges and uncertainties, Abraham's faith was rewarded, and he became the father of many nations, a key part of God's plan for humanity.

Another powerful case study is the life of Moses. Moses was chosen by God to lead the Israelites out of slavery in Egypt, a pivotal moment in God's plan of redemption. Despite his initial reluctance and the many obstacles he faced, Moses' obedience and faithfulness played a crucial role in the fulfillment of God's promises to His people.

In more contemporary times, we can see God's plan at work in the lives of people like Martin Luther King Jr., who, inspired by his Christian faith, played a significant role in advancing civil rights in the United States. His life and work reflect the principles of justice, love, and reconciliation that are central to God's eternal plan.

Comparative Analysis

When comparing the understanding of God's eternal plan across different Christian denominations, we see both similarities and differences. For example, Catholic, Orthodox, and Protestant traditions all affirm the belief in God's sovereign plan, but they may differ in their interpretations of certain aspects of that plan, such as the role of the Church, the nature of salvation, and the understanding of eschatology (the study of the end times).

Catholics, for example, emphasize the role of the Church as the mediator of God's grace and the importance of the sacraments in the believer's journey toward salvation. Orthodox Christians also emphasize the Church's role but focus more on the process of theosis, or becoming one with God, as the ultimate goal of the Christian life.

Protestants, on the other hand, often emphasize the doctrine of sola fide (faith alone), teaching that salvation is through faith in Christ alone, without the need for intermediaries. This belief is central to many Protestant denominations, such as Baptists, Lutherans, and Presbyterians.

Despite these differences, all these traditions share a common belief in God's eternal plan and the hope of eternal life through Jesus Christ.

Deep Dive Exercises

1. Reflect on your understanding of God's eternal plan. How does this understanding shape your daily life and decisions? Write a journal entry exploring how your faith influences your goals, relationships, and sense of purpose.
2. Study the life of a biblical figure such as Abraham, Moses, or David. How did their understanding of God's plan influence their actions and decisions? What can you learn from their faith journey that applies to your own life?

3. Consider how your local church or faith community participates in God's eternal plan. What specific ministries or outreach programs reflect God's love and purpose? How can you get involved or support these efforts?

Personal Reflection and Application

Take some time to reflect on how your life fits into God's eternal plan. What gifts and talents has God given you, and how can you use them to serve His purposes? Consider the areas of your life where you might need to surrender more fully to God's will. Are there aspects of your life where you've been trying to go your own way, rather than seeking God's direction?

Think about how understanding God's eternal plan gives you hope and confidence in the future. How does this knowledge help you navigate the challenges and uncertainties of life? Reflect on the ways you can share this hope with others, whether through words of encouragement, acts of service, or simply living out your faith in a way that others can see.

Expert Insights

Theologians and biblical scholars often emphasize the importance of understanding the big picture of God's plan. N.T. Wright, for example, has written extensively on how the entire Bible tells the story of God's plan to rescue and renew His creation. He argues that understanding this narrative is key to living out the Christian faith in a meaningful way.

Another expert, John Piper, has written about the sovereignty of God and how understanding God's control over all things can bring peace and confidence to believers. Piper often emphasizes that God's ultimate plan is for His glory and our good, and that trusting in this plan is the foundation of a strong and resilient faith.

Discussion and Debate

Engage in discussions with others about the nature of God's eternal plan. Some questions to consider include: How do we reconcile the existence of evil and suffering with God's plan? What is the role of free will in God's sovereign plan? How can believers balance trust in God's plan with taking personal responsibility for their actions?

Debate the different interpretations of key eschatological events, such as the rapture, the tribulation, and the millennium. How do these different views impact the way believers live out their faith? What are the implications for how we understand the mission of the Church and the believer's role in the world?

Practical Tools and Resources

- Books: "*The Purpose Driven Life*" by Rick Warren, "*Knowing God*" by J.I. Packer, "*Desiring God*" by John Piper.
- Online Courses: Courses on biblical theology, eschatology, and Christian living offered by institutions like Dallas Theological Seminary, Gordon-Conwell Theological Seminary, and The Gospel Coalition.
- Study Guides: "*The Story: Getting to the Heart of God's Story*" by Randy Frazee and Max Lucado.
- Church Resources: Join a small group or Bible study focused on

understanding God's plan and how it applies to daily life.

Summary of Insights

In this chapter, we have explored the foundational elements of God's eternal plan and how it provides a framework for understanding our purpose in life. By studying the lives of biblical figures, comparing different Christian traditions, and reflecting on personal application, we gain a deeper understanding of how God's plan unfolds in our lives and the world. The insights gained here are not just theological concepts but practical guides for living a life of faith, hope, and purpose. Understanding God's eternal plan is not just about knowing what will happen in the future, but about living in a way that reflects God's love and purposes today.

Chapter 2: Heaven's Timeline: Unraveling the Future Events

Summary and Key Takeaways

Heaven's timeline is a critical aspect of Christian eschatology, providing believers with a framework for understanding future events according to biblical prophecy. This chapter explores the key milestones in God's plan for the future, from the return of Christ to the final establishment of God's kingdom.

The timeline of heaven, as described in the Bible, includes several significant events:

1. **The Return of Christ:** The Second Coming of Jesus Christ is a central event in Christian eschatology. It signifies the end of the current age and the beginning of a new era

where Christ will establish His kingdom on earth.

2. **The Great Tribulation:** This period, described in the Book of Revelation, is characterized by intense suffering and upheaval. It is a time of trial and testing for humanity, leading up to the final judgment.

3. **The Millennial Reign:** Following the tribulation, Christ will reign for a thousand years, known as the Millennium. This period is marked by peace and justice, as Christ establishes His rule on earth.

4. **The Final Judgment:** At the end of the Millennium, there will be a final judgment where all individuals will be judged according to their deeds. This will lead to the final separation of the righteous from the wicked.

5. **The New Heaven and New Earth:** The final phase of God's plan

involves the creation of a new heaven and a new earth, where God will dwell with His people forever, free from sin and suffering.

One key takeaway is the assurance that God's plan is not arbitrary but follows a divine timeline that will be fulfilled according to His will. Understanding this timeline helps believers live with hope and anticipation, knowing that their current struggles are temporary and that a glorious future awaits.

Another takeaway is the importance of being prepared for these future events. Believers are called to live righteously, share the gospel, and remain vigilant as they await Christ's return. This preparation involves both spiritual readiness and active engagement in God's mission on earth.

Real-Life Case Studies

Understanding heaven's timeline can be illuminated through real-life stories and experiences that reflect the anticipation and preparation for future events. For example, the experience of early Christians facing persecution and martyrdom provides a powerful illustration of living with hope in the midst of trials. Despite their suffering, early Christians held fast to the promise of Christ's return and the ultimate victory of God's kingdom.

In more recent times, movements like the global missions effort reflect the belief in the urgency of preparing for Christ's return. Organizations such as The Billy Graham Evangelistic Association and similar ministries focus on spreading the message of salvation worldwide, driven by the belief that Christ's return is imminent and that the Great Commission is a vital part of God's timeline.

Another case study is the impact of end-times teaching on personal and communal practices. For example, individuals and churches that emphasize eschatological teachings often engage in prayer, fasting, and outreach activities as expressions of their anticipation of Christ's return. These practices demonstrate the intersection of belief and action in preparing for future events.

Comparative Analysis

Different Christian traditions interpret the timeline of heaven in various ways, reflecting their theological perspectives. For instance:

- **Premillennialism:** This view holds that Christ will return before the Millennium to establish His kingdom on earth. Premillennialists often emphasize a literal interpretation of the Book of Revelation and believe in a pre-tribulation rapture of the Church.
- **Postmillennialism:** Postmillennialists believe that Christ will return after the Millennium, which will be established through the gradual influence of the gospel on the world. This view often emphasizes the transformative power of the Church in society.
- **Amillennialism:** Amillennialists interpret the Millennium symbolically, seeing it as the current church age. According to this view, Christ's reign is spiritual rather than physical, and the timeline of heaven

is understood in a more symbolic or allegorical sense.

Despite these differences, all these traditions agree on the ultimate hope of Christ's return and the establishment of God's eternal kingdom. Comparing these perspectives helps believers understand the diversity of interpretations and find common ground in their shared hope for the future.

Deep Dive Exercises

1. **Study the Book of Revelation:** Read selected passages from the Book of Revelation that describe the end times. Create a timeline of key events based on your reading and summarize their significance in the context of heaven's timeline.

2. **Examine Historical and Contemporary Views:** Research

different theological perspectives on the timeline of heaven, such as premillennialism, postmillennialism, and amillennialism. Write a comparative analysis of these views and their implications for Christian living.

3. **Create a Personal End-Times Plan:** Based on your understanding of heaven's timeline, develop a personal plan for spiritual preparation. This might include setting specific goals for prayer, Bible study, and involvement in church activities that align with your eschatological beliefs.

Personal Reflection and Application

Reflect on how the timeline of heaven impacts your personal faith and daily life. How does the anticipation of Christ's return and the ultimate fulfillment of God's promises influence your priorities and decisions? Consider how the promise of a new heaven and new earth shapes your understanding of suffering and hope in the present.

Think about how you can actively prepare for future events. Are there areas of your life where you need to make changes or take specific actions in light of the coming timeline? Reflect on how your faith in these future events can inspire you to live a life that reflects God's kingdom values.

Expert Insights

Theologians and biblical scholars provide valuable insights into the timeline of heaven. For example, Wayne Grudem's *"Systematic Theology"* offers a comprehensive overview of eschatological views and their implications for Christian doctrine and practice. Grudem's work emphasizes the importance of understanding biblical prophecy in the context of God's overall plan.

Another expert, John Stott, has written extensively on the nature of Christian hope and the impact of eschatology on practical living. Stott's writings highlight the relevance of end-times teachings for contemporary Christians and the importance of living with an eternal perspective.

Discussion and Debate

Engage in discussions about the implications of different interpretations of heaven's timeline. Some questions to consider include: How does your understanding of the end times affect your view of current events and global issues? What role does eschatology play in shaping the mission and priorities of the Church?

Debate the practical implications of various eschatological views. For example, how does the belief in a pre-tribulation rapture influence a believer's approach to evangelism and social justice? How does a postmillennial perspective impact the way Christians engage with cultural and societal issues?

Practical Tools and Resources

- Books: *"The Last Days According to Jesus"* by R.C. Sproul, *"Revelation: Four Views: A Parallel Commentary"* by Steve Gregg, *"Kingdom Come: The Amillennial Alternative"* by Sam Storms.
- Online Courses: Courses on eschatology and biblical prophecy offered by institutions such as The

Gospel Coalition, Ligonier
Ministries, and Moody Bible
Institute.

- Study Guides: *"The Book of
Revelation: A Commentary"* by G.K.
Beale, *"Understanding End Times
Prophecy"* by Paul Benware.
- Church Resources: Engage in Bible
studies or small groups focused on
eschatology and heaven's timeline.

Summary of Insights

This chapter has explored the timeline of
heaven, providing a framework for
understanding future events according to
biblical prophecy. By examining the key
milestones, comparing different
theological perspectives, and reflecting
on practical applications, believers gain a
deeper understanding of how God's plan
for the future unfolds. The insights gained

from this study offer both hope and guidance, helping believers live in anticipation of Christ's return and the ultimate fulfillment of God's promises.

Chapter 3: The Rapture and Tribulation: A Deep Dive into Prophetic Milestones

Summary and Key Takeaways

The concepts of the Rapture and the Tribulation are central to many Christian eschatological frameworks, representing significant milestones in the timeline of heaven. Understanding these events helps believers grasp the broader narrative of God's plan and their role within it.

The Rapture

The Rapture refers to the event when believers are caught up to meet Christ in the air, as described in 1 Thessalonians 4:16-17. This event is often associated with the end times and is interpreted differently across various theological traditions:

1. **Pre-Tribulation Rapture:** This view holds that the Rapture will occur before the Great Tribulation, allowing believers to escape the suffering and judgment that will follow. Proponents of this view argue that the Church will be spared from the trials described in the Book of Revelation.

2. **Mid-Tribulation Rapture:** According to this perspective, the Rapture will take place in the middle of the Tribulation period. Believers will experience the initial phase of suffering but will be taken up before the most intense judgments occur.

3. **Post-Tribulation Rapture:** This view suggests that the Rapture will occur at the end of the Tribulation, with believers enduring the full period of suffering before being gathered to Christ. This perspective emphasizes

the endurance of faith through trials.

The Tribulation

The Tribulation is a period of intense suffering and turmoil that will precede the Second Coming of Christ. It is characterized by various events:

1. **The Seal Judgments:** These are a series of judgments described in Revelation 6, where each seal opened by Christ results in a different calamity affecting the earth.
2. **The Trumpet Judgments:** Following the seal judgments, the trumpet judgments (Revelation 8-9) involve further disasters and plagues that impact the world.
3. **The Bowl Judgments:** The final set of judgments, known as the bowl

judgments, are described in Revelation 16. They represent the culmination of God's wrath and lead up to the final battle between good and evil.

Key takeaways include the understanding that the Rapture and Tribulation are integral to the unfolding of God's plan for the end times. They reflect the themes of divine justice and mercy, with the Rapture offering hope for believers and the Tribulation serving as a period of testing and purification.

Real-Life Case Studies

Real-life case studies provide context for how these prophetic events impact believers and their faith:

1. **Historical Persecution:** Throughout history, Christians have faced

persecution and suffering, which some interpret as a foreshadowing of the Tribulation. The experiences of early Christians under Roman rule or more recent examples of persecution in regions like the Middle East highlight the endurance of faith in the face of trials.

2. **Modern-Day Evangelicalism:** The belief in the Rapture and Tribulation has influenced contemporary evangelical movements. For example, the Left Behind series by Tim LaHaye and Jerry B. Jenkins reflects popular interpretations of these events and has impacted the way many Christians view the end times.

3. **Church Responses to Crisis:** Churches and Christian organizations often use teachings on the Rapture and Tribulation to

prepare believers spiritually and practically for times of crisis. Efforts to support persecuted Christians and promote faith-based resilience demonstrate the practical application of these eschatological concepts.

Comparative Analysis

Different Christian traditions offer varying interpretations of the Rapture and Tribulation, reflecting their broader theological perspectives:

- **Dispensationalism:** This approach, popular among some evangelical Christians, includes a detailed timeline of end-times events, including a pre-Tribulation Rapture. Dispensationalists often emphasize a literal interpretation of the Bible and distinguish between Israel and the Church.

- **Historic Premillennialism:** Historic premillennialists also anticipate a period of Tribulation but generally do not adhere to a specific Rapture event before the Tribulation. They view the Church's suffering as part of the end times.
- **Amillennialism:** Amillennialists interpret the Tribulation symbolically and see the Rapture as a metaphor for the final victory of Christ. They do not emphasize a literal seven-year Tribulation period.

Comparing these perspectives helps believers understand the diversity of interpretations and the reasons behind them. Each tradition offers insights into how Christians can prepare for and understand the end times.

Deep Dive Exercises

1. **Study Revelation Passages:** Read
   and analyze the passages in the
   Book of Revelation that describe the
   Rapture and Tribulation. Create a
   summary of each judgment and its
   significance in the overall narrative.

2. **Compare Rapture Views:** Research
   the different views on the Rapture
   (pre-, mid-, and post-Tribulation)
   and write a comparative analysis.
   Discuss how each view impacts the
   understanding of God's plan and the
   believer's role.

3. **Develop a Personal Response Plan:**
   Based on your understanding of the
   Rapture and Tribulation, create a
   plan for spiritual preparedness. This
   plan might include setting goals for
   prayer, studying Scripture, and
   engaging in community support.

Personal Reflection and Application

Reflect on how the concepts of the Rapture and Tribulation influence your personal faith and daily life. How does the anticipation of these events affect your priorities and actions? Consider how the promise of the Rapture and the reality of the Tribulation shape your understanding of suffering and hope.

Evaluate how you can prepare spiritually and practically for the challenges described in these events. What steps can you take to strengthen your faith and support others in their spiritual journey?

Expert Insights

Scholars and theologians provide valuable perspectives on the Rapture and Tribulation:

- **John Walvoord:** As a prominent dispensationalist theologian, Walvoord's writings offer insights into the pre-Tribulation Rapture and its implications for Christian living. His book *"The Rapture Question"* provides a comprehensive overview of the topic.
- **N.T. Wright:** Wright's work on New Testament theology offers a different perspective on eschatology, emphasizing the symbolic and historical aspects of the Tribulation. His book *"Simply Jesus"* explores the broader context of Jesus' teachings on the end times.

Discussion and Debate

Engage in discussions about the implications of different interpretations of the Rapture and Tribulation. Consider questions such as: How do various views impact the Church's mission and outreach efforts? What role do these beliefs play in shaping personal and communal practices?

Debate the practical implications of the Rapture and Tribulation. For example, how does the belief in a pre-Tribulation Rapture influence Christian engagement with societal issues? How does a post-Tribulation perspective affect the way Christians prepare for and respond to crises?

Practical Tools and Resources

- Books: *"The Rapture Question"* by John Walvoord, *"Simply Jesus"* by N.T. Wright, *"Revelation: The Countdown to the Second Coming"* by Hal Lindsey.

- Online Courses: Courses on eschatology and biblical prophecy offered by institutions such as Dallas Theological Seminary and The Gospel Coalition.
- Study Guides: *"The Book of Revelation: A Commentary"* by G.K. Beale, *"Understanding End Times Prophecy"* by Paul Benware.
- Church Resources: Engage in Bible studies or small groups focused on the Rapture and Tribulation.

Summary of Insights

This chapter has delved into the Rapture and Tribulation, offering a comprehensive understanding of these prophetic milestones. By examining different interpretations, real-life case studies, and practical applications, believers gain a deeper insight into how these events fit into the broader timeline of heaven. The study of these concepts provides both hope and preparedness, helping believers navigate their faith in anticipation of the future.

Chapter 4: The Millennium: Reigning with Christ in the Golden Era

Summary and Key Takeaways

The concept of the Millennium is a significant aspect of Christian eschatology, referring to a future thousand-year reign of Christ on earth as described in Revelation 20:1-6. This period is often envisioned as a time of peace, righteousness, and fulfillment of God's promises. Understanding the Millennium helps believers anticipate the culmination of God's redemptive plan and the restoration of creation.

The Millennium: Key Concepts

1. **Biblical Description:** Revelation 20:1-6 describes the Millennium as a time when Christ will reign with His saints for a thousand years. During

this period, Satan will be bound, and there will be a time of peace and justice on earth.

2. **Premillennialism:** This view holds that Christ will return before the Millennium and establish His reign on earth. Premillennialists interpret the Millennium as a literal, future reign of Christ that will follow a period of great tribulation.

3. **Postmillennialism:** Postmillennialists believe that the Millennium represents a golden age of the Church's influence and spiritual progress leading up to Christ's return. This view sees the Millennium as a symbolic period that has been unfolding throughout history, culminating in Christ's Second Coming.

4. **Amillennialism:** Amillennialists interpret the Millennium

metaphorically, viewing it as the current church age. According to this perspective, Christ's reign is spiritual and occurs in the hearts of believers rather than through a literal, earthly kingdom.

Key Takeaways:

- The Millennium is central to the Christian hope for a restored world and divine justice.
- Different theological perspectives offer varying interpretations of how and when the Millennium will occur.
- The anticipation of the Millennium influences Christian understanding of present struggles and future expectations.

Real-Life Case Studies

1. **Historic Premillennialism:** Early Christian writings, such as those of the Church Fathers, reflect premillennial beliefs. The work of theologians like Irenaeus and Justin Martyr provides insights into how early Christians understood the Millennium.

2. **Postmillennial Influence:** The influence of postmillennial thought is evident in the work of historical figures such as Jonathan Edwards, who envisioned the Millennium as a time of great spiritual revival and societal transformation.

3. **Amillennial Perspectives:** Modern amillennialism, represented by theologians like Augustine and modern scholars, offers a symbolic interpretation of the Millennium. This perspective emphasizes the

present spiritual reign of Christ and the ongoing work of the Church.

Comparative Analysis

Different theological traditions offer unique perspectives on the Millennium, each with implications for understanding Christ's reign and the nature of the kingdom:

- **Premillennialism vs. Postmillennialism:** Premillennialism anticipates a literal, future reign of Christ, while postmillennialism sees the Millennium as a period of increasing Christian influence leading up to Christ's return. This comparison highlights differing views on the nature of Christ's kingdom and the role of the Church in shaping history.

- **Amillennialism:** Amillennialism contrasts with premillennial and postmillennial views by interpreting the Millennium as a present spiritual reality. This perspective emphasizes the ongoing reign of Christ in the lives of believers rather than a future, earthly kingdom.

Understanding these perspectives helps believers appreciate the diversity of thought within Christian eschatology and provides a broader view of how different traditions interpret the concept of the Millennium.

Deep Dive Exercises

1. **Study Revelation 20:** Read Revelation 20:1-6 and analyze the text in light of different millennial perspectives. Summarize how each view interprets this passage and its

implications for understanding Christ's reign.

2. **Explore Historical Figures:** Research historical figures who have influenced the interpretation of the Millennium, such as Irenaeus, Augustine, and Jonathan Edwards. Write a brief overview of their contributions and how their views shaped Christian eschatology.

3. **Develop a Personal Vision:** Based on your study of the Millennium, develop a personal vision of what the reign of Christ means for your faith and practice. Consider how this vision impacts your understanding of God's promises and your role in His plan.

Personal Reflection and Application

Reflect on how the concept of the Millennium influences your understanding of God's plan and your place within it. Consider the following questions:

- How does the anticipation of the Millennium shape your expectations for the future?
- In what ways can you align your life with the values and principles of Christ's kingdom?
- How can the hope of the Millennium provide comfort and motivation in your current circumstances?

Evaluate how the different interpretations of the Millennium impact your faith and daily life. Consider how understanding these perspectives can enhance your spiritual growth and influence your approach to challenges.

Expert Insights

Scholars and theologians offer valuable insights into the concept of the Millennium:

- **John Stott:** A prominent evangelical theologian, Stott's work on eschatology provides insights into the different millennial views and their implications for Christian living. His book *"The Last Days"* explores various interpretations of the Millennium and their impact on faith.
- **G.K. Beale:** Beale's scholarly work on Revelation offers a comprehensive analysis of the Millennium and its significance in the broader context of biblical prophecy. His commentary *"The Book of Revelation: A Commentary"* provides in-depth

insights into the text and its interpretations.

Discussion and Debate

Engage in discussions about the implications of different millennial views for the Church and individual believers. Consider questions such as:

- How do different interpretations of the Millennium impact the Church's mission and outreach efforts?
- What role does the concept of the Millennium play in shaping Christian hope and expectations?

Debate the practical implications of the Millennium for contemporary Christian living. For example, how does the anticipation of Christ's reign influence ethical decision-making and social engagement?

Practical Tools and Resources

- Books: *"The Last Days"* by John Stott, *"The Book of Revelation: A Commentary"* by G.K. Beale, *"Three Views on the Millennium and Beyond"* edited by Darrell L. Bock.
- Online Courses: Courses on eschatology and millennial views offered by institutions such as Wheaton College and The Gospel Coalition.
- Study Guides: *"A Commentary on the Revelation of John"* by Robert H. Mounce, *"The Millennium and Beyond"* by Michael J. Vlach.
- Church Resources: Engage in Bible studies or small groups focused on eschatology and the Millennium.

Summary of Insights

This chapter has explored the concept of the Millennium, providing a comprehensive understanding of its significance and implications. By examining different theological perspectives, real-life case studies, and practical applications, believers gain a deeper insight into Christ's future reign and its impact on their faith. The study of the Millennium offers hope and perspective for navigating the present and anticipating the future.

Chapter 5: Living with Hope: Preparing for What Happens Next

Summary and Key Takeaways

Living with hope in the context of Christian eschatology involves understanding and preparing for the future as outlined in the Bible. Max Lucado's *What Happens Next* emphasizes the importance of hope and preparation in facing the future with faith and confidence. This chapter explores practical ways to live with hope, drawing on biblical principles and Lucado's insights.

Key Concepts in Living with Hope:

1. **Biblical Hope:** Hope in the Christian context is more than wishful thinking; it is a confident expectation based on God's

promises. This hope is rooted in the belief that God has a plan for the future and that His promises will be fulfilled.

2. **Preparation Through Faith:** Preparing for the future involves cultivating a strong faith that trusts in God's plan. This preparation includes spiritual readiness, understanding biblical prophecy, and living according to Christian values.

3. **Practical Living:** Living with hope means integrating this hope into daily life. It involves making choices that reflect faith, engaging in practices that strengthen one's relationship with God, and actively participating in the mission of the Church.

4. **Community Support:** The support of a Christian community plays a

crucial role in sustaining hope. Engaging with fellow believers provides encouragement, accountability, and a shared sense of purpose.

Key Takeaways:

- Hope is an essential aspect of the Christian life, providing strength and direction as believers navigate the future.
- Preparation involves both spiritual and practical aspects, including understanding God's promises and living in alignment with them.
- Community support enhances personal hope and contributes to collective spiritual growth.

Real-Life Case Studies

1. **Hope in Crisis:** The experience of Christians during times of crisis, such as the early Church's persecution or modern instances of religious persecution, illustrates how hope sustains faith through hardship. Stories of believers who have maintained their faith in dire circumstances provide inspiration and insight into living with hope.

2. **Community and Support:** Examples from Christian communities that have effectively supported members through challenges demonstrate the power of collective hope. Initiatives such as prayer groups, support networks, and charitable actions show how communities can foster hope and prepare for the future.

3. **Personal Transformation:** Individuals who have experienced significant personal transformation

through faith provide real-life examples of how hope can lead to profound changes. Their stories highlight the impact of hope on personal growth and resilience.

Comparative Analysis

Comparing the Christian concept of hope with other religious or secular views provides a broader perspective on living with hope:

- **Christian Hope vs. Secular Optimism:** Christian hope is based on divine promises and a relationship with God, whereas secular optimism relies on human efforts and societal progress. Understanding these differences helps clarify the unique aspects of Christian hope.

- **Interfaith Perspectives:** Exploring how hope is understood in different religious traditions, such as Islam or Judaism, offers insights into common themes and distinct differences. This comparison highlights the role of hope in various faith contexts and its significance in the Christian tradition.

Deep Dive Exercises

1. **Scripture Study:** Select passages related to hope, such as Romans 15:13 or 1 Peter 1:3-5. Reflect on these verses and write about how they shape your understanding of hope and preparation for the future.

2. **Personal Action Plan:** Develop a plan for incorporating hope into your daily life. Include specific actions such as prayer, Bible study,

and community involvement. Evaluate how these actions align with your understanding of biblical hope.

3. **Community Engagement:** Identify ways to support and encourage others within your Christian community. Consider organizing a group study, participating in outreach programs, or offering personal support to those in need.

Personal Reflection and Application

Reflect on how the concept of hope influences your daily life and spiritual journey. Consider the following questions:

- How does your understanding of hope impact your response to challenges and uncertainties?

- In what ways can you actively prepare for the future while maintaining hope in God's promises?
- How can you contribute to fostering hope within your community and supporting others in their faith journeys?

Evaluate how your personal experiences with hope align with the biblical principles discussed. Reflect on areas where you can enhance your preparation and integration of hope into your life.

Expert Insights

Experts provide valuable perspectives on the role of hope in the Christian life:

- **Tim Keller:** In his book *"Hope in Times of Fear,"* Keller explores the significance of hope in the face of adversity and how it shapes the

Christian experience. His insights offer practical advice on living with hope in challenging times.

- **N.T. Wright:** Wright's writings on Christian hope and eschatology, including "*Surprised by Hope*," provide a theological framework for understanding hope in the context of God's promises and the future.

Discussion and Debate

Engage in discussions about the role of hope in the Christian life and its practical implications:

- How does the concept of hope influence your understanding of God's plan and your role in it?
- What are the challenges and rewards of living with hope in a world that often seems uncertain or hostile to faith?

Debate the impact of hope on personal and communal aspects of faith. Consider how different interpretations of hope affect Christian practice and the broader mission of the Church.

Practical Tools and Resources

- Books: "*Hope in Times of Fear*" by Tim Keller, "*Surprised by Hope*" by N.T. Wright, "*The Power of Hope*" by Richard G. W. Smith.
- Online Courses: Courses on Christian hope and eschatology offered by institutions such as The Gospel Coalition and BiblicalTraining.org.
- Study Guides: "*Hope: A Biblical Perspective*" by John Piper, "*Living with Hope*" by David Jeremiah.
- Community Resources: Engage in church programs and groups

focused on fostering hope and spiritual growth.

Summary of Insights

This chapter has explored the practical aspects of living with hope, emphasizing the importance of preparation, community support, and personal reflection. By understanding and applying the concept of hope, believers can navigate the future with confidence and align their lives with God's promises. The insights and exercises provided aim to equip readers to live with hope and contribute to a hopeful Christian community.

_____

_____

_____

Made in the USA
Las Vegas, NV
04 November 2024

11123929R00042